Ant's Hamster

By Tony Bradman

Illustrations by Jon Stuart

OXFORD

UNIVERSITY PRESS

In this story ...

- Introduce children to the characters in this story:
  Ant, Ant's mum and Ant's hamster, Pickles.
- Point to the words that represent the characters' names and
  say each of the names together. Children will meet these
  words in the story.

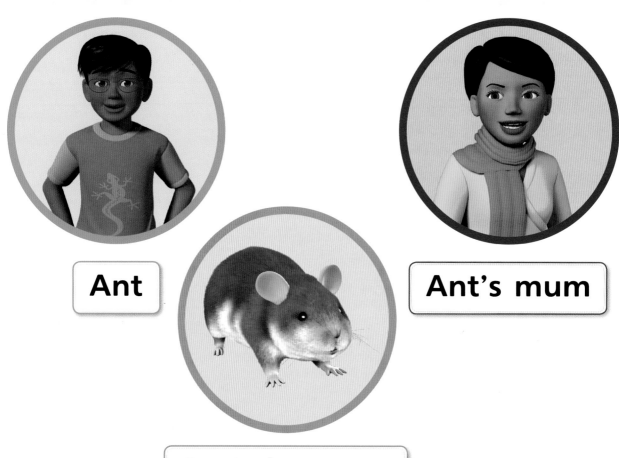

Ant

Ant's mum

Ant's hamster

"Oh no, look at that!" said Mum, pointing at a hole in a cereal box. "A mouse must have got into the kitchen. I'll have to put down a trap."

Ant didn't want the mouse to be caught in a trap. Besides, he had a feeling it wasn't a mouse at all … his hamster Pickles had gone missing earlier that day.

"What a mess!" said Mum. "We need to set a trap."

3

READ

As soon as Ant was on his own, he pushed the button on his watch to shrink to micro-size. He climbed into the kitchen cupboard. It was very messy!

Suddenly, he heard something just ahead of him. Then he saw Pickles disappearing round a corner!

TALK

- Talk about the cupboard. Ask children to think of words to describe what they can see.

ACTIVITY

- Point to the word *wait* on the page and ask children to sound-talk it (i.e. wait becomes w-ai-t).
- Then ask them to blend the sounds together and say the word (i.e. w-ai-t becomes wait).
- Ask children to write the word *wait*. They could use magnetic letters, a whiteboard or a pencil and paper to write.

✦ Tip

See the inside back cover for more guidance on sounds.

4

Ant sees his hamster.
It runs off into a corner.

📖 READ

Ant chased after Pickles, but he lost him. He could hear him scratching but couldn't see him!

"Oh, where are you, Pickles?" said Ant.

💬 TALK

- Ask children where Pickles is hiding in the picture.

👥 ACTIVITY

- Point to the word *hear* and ask children to sound-talk it (i.e. hear becomes h-ear).
- Then ask them to blend the sounds together and say the word (i.e. h-ear becomes hear).
- Ask children to write the word *hear*.
- Ask children to say the last sound in the word *hear* (i.e. the /ear/ sound). Can they think of other words that have the /ear/ sound at the end (e.g. near, fear).

Ant had a torch in his pocket. He shone the light into the corner.

There was Pickles, huddled up and looking scared. "Don't be frightened, Pickles," said Ant. "I'm here to help you."

But the hamster wouldn't come out.

ACTIVITY

- Ask children to write the word *light*.

- Read out the following sentence: *Ant caught sight of Pickles.* Ask children how they would change the word *light* to *sight*.

- Now read out the following sentence: *Pickles got a fright.* How would children change the word *sight* to *fright*.

Now it is light, Ant can see his hamster. "Out you come, little hamster!" said Ant. "Do not be afraid."

📖 READ

Then, Ant had an idea. "I know! I'll tempt you out with some food," he said, spying a box of cereal bars.

Ant ripped open a bar. He tore bits off and offered them to the hamster, walking back towards the cupboard door. "That's it, Pickles … Out you come," he said.

💬 TALK

- Tell children some hamster facts:
  - Hamsters can save food in their cheeks.
  - Hamsters are nocturnal. That means they usually sleep during the day but are awake at night.
  - Hamsters can run very fast and can sometimes even run backwards!

👥 ACTIVITY

- Ask children to count how many letters there are in the word *little*.
- Then ask children to sound-talk the word *little* (i.e. little becomes l-i-tt-le).
- Repeat the activity with the word *hamster*.

Ant drops little bits of food for the hamster. "One bit for you, and one bit for me. Out we go!" said Ant.

📖 READ

Ant had forgotten about the trap that his mum had put down in the cupboard. He knocked against it. The spring pinged and the trap snapped shut. He jumped clear, narrowly missing it.

"Argh!" said Ant. "The sooner I get you out of here the better, Pickles!"

💬 TALK

- Ask children to describe how they think Ant felt when the trap snapped. Use this as an opportunity to extend their vocabulary (e.g. shocked, surprised).

👥 ACTIVITY

- Read out the following sentence and ask children to say the missing word: *Ant jumped back in …* (clue: it rhymes with *sock*). (shock)

Ant picks up his hamster.

📖 READ

Ant climbed out of the cupboard. He pushed the button on his watch and grew back to normal size.

Ant was just coaxing Pickles out of the cupboard when he heard Mum coming down the stairs. "Quick, Pickles! Mum's coming! Don't be scared. You're safe now," said Ant.

💬 TALK

- Ask children to think of a word that describes how Ant felt when he lost Pickles. Can they think of a word to describe how he felt when he got Pickles safely out?

👥 ACTIVITY

- Ask children to write a list of objects they can see in the picture that begin with the /c/ sound (e.g. cooker, cloth). Remind children to sound-talk the words before they write them.

14

READ

Mum came in the kitchen and looked in the cupboard. "What's happened here? The trap has sprung but there's no mouse! It must have got away!"

Ant didn't say a word …

ACTIVITY

- **Have some fun!** Ask children to make up their own stories about a pet that gets lost and tell their stories to a partner.

What did you do?

"Sh! Do not tell!"